Airport music

ALSO BY MARK TARDI:

Euclid Sudders, Brooklyn, NY: Litmus Press, 2003
Part First——Chopin's Feet, Bainbridge Island, WA: g o n g, 2005
Airport music, Milwaukee, WI: Bronze Skull Press, 2005

MARK TARDI

Airport music

Burning Deck/Anyart, Providence

ACKNOWLEDGMENTS:

Excerpts of the book have appeared — sometimes in earlier versions — in *Antennae, Aufgabe, Bird Dog, Boog City, Chicago Review, Conundrum, Play A Journal Of Plays, Traverse, Van Gogh's Ear*; in the anthologies *Chopin with Cherries: A Tribute in Verse*, ed. Maja Trochimczyk, Los Angeles: Moonrise Press, 2010 and *The City Visible: Chicago Poetry for the New Millennium*, ed. Raymond Bianchi & William Allegrezza, Chicago: Cracked Slab Press, 2007; and in the chapbooks *Part First——Chopin's Feet* and *Airport music*.

"Reciprocal of Rain" was origially performed in Brown University's "Once Upon a Weekend" short plays festival, directed by Sarah Ruhl. The cast featured Lucy Boyle, Kamili Feelings, Sawako Nakayasu, a few eggs, glasses of water, a spoon, two chairs, a broom, and a tape recorder.

The author thanks the editors and collaborators for their support.

Burning Deck is the literature program of Anyart: Contemporary Arts Center, a tax-exempt (501c3), non-profit organization.

The cover reproduces Sean Scully's "Return," 2007, Oil on linen, 85 x 75" (215.9 x 190.5 cm), Private Collection, New York, © Sean Scully. Author and publisher thank Sean Scully for his gracious permission.

ISBN13: 978-1-936194-14-8, original paperback

To my family,
forever between here and there

In Memoriam
Henry and Mary Grzesiak

Contents

October

It remains: a severed variable, still steps
or walking ash, an étude of

This is the way they describe H:

Nobody sits.

The cloud cataracts the lake.

In the porches of my ear.

False lull. Refracted.

It becomes time to inquire.

Almost a corridor.

Insect rays. Refusing night.

as the rain began to write

radiant silence
baroquely cloaked

bloodhours

strolls at the sloping dusk
lost pools of

Now is a paradox.

Buried nets of a thousand knots.

"They are innocent at their neutral equations."

    ghost leticuli
    unangled

a thing out in the waves

dreamt off

That I saw. Saw
antithesis nod twice.

The position of cinder to ribs
dust breedings, alley apples

Yesterday the girl in the adjoining room. Skin swept. Expectant.

Everything that surrounds. An unlike night. Leaves without knees breathing like some sort of bed.

The simplest rations. Tray to beam.

Let us try to make a pledge in our sleep.

Three days. Unpronounced.

The cemetery no longer.

Now a five-footed thing without offspring.

As I forgot my face.

Furtively silent.

Salt steps they knew.

Three weeks. Third hint.

Because neither water nor shadow.

Like these out of hand.

The almost of every Saturday.

A better word for want.

Cycle down. Called and polished.

Jogfry for the misremembered.

"I have eight sculptors' heads swimming in my name."

And the yellow line in the and the yellow line.

Only chairs outside of sleep.

General thirst. Waltz without shadow.

Up or down or to speak.

The dust of questions (coughing out).

Plastic clarity. Peeled snow.

Here there are little veins.

Unconsoled exits changing hands.

the same indifferent sun

those splinters
stitched along the border

seat of the affections

blameless
another for the wind to

Shortly probably means to shave two days.

Just nice time to walk to Artane.

Streets of their brow. All night and net.

And this a new face.

The nine-dimensional fracture.

Or string desperate for.

Disappear in the direction of the bridge.
That owned accident.
Instant of blind but. Silent.
Sentried in the corner.

Back in the city it can't last.
The sky color of nickel.
Your particular solvencies. Sickroom talents.
All dead names.
Every debarkation an attack.

The opposite in empty. Possible fires.

That is to say *All looked.*

An algorithm for rain.

Failures I used to sleep.

Airport music

Nothing will absolve you of yourself. Not the train tracks a block away, not *zimne piwo* or carefully manicured lawns, not the chairs that guard our parking spots, a cigarette necktie.

Let x equal the amount of broken glass strewn across the sidewalk;

Let y equal the most hurried, the last

this brute contingency

that any breathing falls, imperfect
half-boarded up

There's no harm for anyone else
in your mathematics

thin negatives,
slant black

never quiet, only graspless

locked into the cut of a house

Let k equal a knot of people, expectant
sounding each other out

a drawn bath to deform water

a butcher's broom

Second letter on the same day:

Best to end these confidences. It's not that I'm superstitious, but that I'm not. Some people like to go to church, and some people like cherries. A corpse won't change any of that. The usual whisper and splash, soup and a pair of shoes.

That streets are sewn together.

Nose bleed en route.

Tray to beam.

That steak weapons.

To your desolate without.

Private fire trucks.

It's an insurance job.

Softball without gloves.

A leg laugh.

The Calumet Record, October 1907:

12 died in the neighborhood of the blast furnace;
3 were electrocuted;
1 died in a dynamite accident;
3 fell from a high place;
4 were struck by a falling object;
4 were killed by hot metal in the Bessemer department;
3 were crushed to death;
1 was suffocated by gas;
1 was thrown from a high place by the wind;
1 was scorched to death by a hot slag;
10 were killed by railroad cars or locomotives.

Still no solution, so how about an old joke:

2 plus 2 equals 5 for *sufficiently large* values of 2.

Maybe you're right that the infinite resembles a wound, but "unperturbed kernels radiant and inevitable?"

Yes, I know counting is not proving. So I'm left reaching.
If you're dead, do let me know.

Yes, ruthless
so much a square mile

pickled hands and cutworm

Yes, clean geometries
successed,

warned with corners

A stuffed
zero in an armchair

poorly equipped for the cold

Your algebra nearly fainted, salt-blue

The question of specific gravity

baths filling, flagpoles
casting shadows,

your father's negative age

five years ago

5 out of 4 people have trouble with fractions.
The entireness of simple touch. All those
lost landscapes.

Your dead body looks like rain;

Mine, rotted planks for pavement, standing
water, vinegar, another flu out of season

Don't ask how we went, by what sudden leap
or what unforeseen modulation. This zero with
so many ciphers.

It was impossible to watch:

To undress and dress again.
The chest a harpsichord.

That the withheld is the only eloquence left.

Flags and bunting everywhere.

A built-in lefthandedness.

Woven wind.

That the dead are protected.

Another infinity, a hotel.

It was an injury to the idea.

A saucepan to plant some flowers in.

I was born 99 years after
Mordecai Brown

in a container of light

With all my fingers

Each time the world exists
a little more for us

not an area code or insult

southwind pretending Warsaw

A number in a tree,
grey octaves, eigen values

going into the future backwards

And especially the edge, chromatic nuance

now particle, now wave

sad toothed

the condition for every

To pitch, to interior.
To undress and dress again.

My back to your fidgeting.
To cut square.

The actual mountain.
Blind radius, the static field.

Explicitly, no.
The palace of the mouth.

To particle without.
To merely hold your cell, stainless.

Threaded.
Light-safe if not repose.

A bathroom above it.

Instead of splinters, certainties

Wine is wet fire;
stone coagulated dust

I know that I love my mother—and yours

and some days that's almost enough

Czarnina

1. Purchase duck and blood from butcher. The blood will contain vinegar. (If preparing own poultry, put 1/2 cup vinegar into glass bowl with blood to prevent coagulation. Set aside.)

2. Cover duck and back ribs with water in a large kettle. Add salt. Bring to boil. Skim off foam.

3. Put celery, parsley, allspice, and cloves into cheesecloth bag and add to soup. Cover and cook over low heat until meat is tender (about 1 1/2 hours).

4. Remove spice bag from kettle. Discard bones, cut up meat. Return meat to soup. Add prunes, raisins, and apple (if desired); mix. Cook 30 minutes.

5. With beater, blend flour and sugar into cream until smooth. Then add blood mixture, a little at a time, continuing to beat.

6. Add about 1/2 cup hot soup stock to blood mixture, blending thoroughly. Pour mixture slowly into soup, stirring constantly until soup comes just to boiling.

7. Season to taste with salt, pepper, and lemon juice or vinegar. Serve with homemade noodles, if desired.

A you, cast in lost matter

Stacked tiles,
          cuttooth

as though the ridden wore nothing

no starfoot fibula,
fenced in

no contact mines

salt ready to tear the light

That the heat hangs itself inside you

That the scales had fallen from their eyes

Carved their own statue

That any question is a question of angle

That we're older than our lives

A drop of air, dragged, bridge-strung

Not red, but late orange

failed into a street

I wouldn't be somewhere else

I wouldn't just look,

inherit a postcard

on the spindle side

Only mornings

Fewer breakdowns, insomniacs

the fear it seduces

Who had scars above
his eyes. Who opened them.
Who exchanged visits
on Sundays. Who brought
an egg on Easter. Who
expired the day before.

Who bit whose ass. Whose
stitches split. Who called
California. Who cracked the table.
Whose knees went in 'Nam.

Who loved the purple clown. Who
hated clothes. Who wasn't drunk.
Who was at every game.

Who stayed.

They were entire functions, quasi doubly periodic, q-series, mock theta

And they were the future behaved at infinity

open air rooms, inescapable
starboard

Vitamin D deficient

A bad year for scarves,
broken symmetries, those thin potato soups

which were the beginning

And they were blue almonds or heavy hydrogen

very much a jump in the dark
buried and buried again

Your plastic itinerary, a loss cone
lying in wait

We remain equal to

ourselves in a container of light. More half-open lips
across a handkerchief, that desperate calendar

If my story's a trauma, yours is too. October bending
at its edge: bloodwind, parietal, bed-shaped

a drop of air implacably kinetic.

Silence as in a runway

Reciprocal of Rain

Characters: There must be at least zero characters.

Dialogue: May be stage directions.

Stage Directions: May be dialogue.

Setting: At a particular time. In a particular place. Or thereabouts.

Note: The scenes may be performed in any order.

I don't think the lake slept   ∫

                    ∫   To step away from the air

Like an étude   ∫

∫   Inscribed on the wrist

That isn't to say   ∫

            ∫   It all wearies the hand

These numbered days   ∫

∫   But I can't seem to recall

The sound of its face   ∫

            ∫   Holes that are really shoes

As if it simply stood there

Slung on a shadow

Limbless

A long wash

Distant whispers

You didn't use a ladder

In any month

It all seems so clear now

To dance without motion

Mirrors made of string

:Dear Quadrature

:Dear Intentional-or-Unintentional-Town

:Dear Chopin's-Feet

:Dear Seat-of-the-Affections

:Dear Laddered-Light

:Dear Scissors

:Dear Forty-Seven

:Dear This-Tea-Might-Do-the-Trick

:Dear Walking-Ash

:Dear *Czarnina*

They keep perfectly / Undoing the strings / Off a measure / You seem uncertain/
Elegant scrapes / Subtracting rain / Nor the absence of fuel / False lull /
The instance where /

Again overnight diminished

Perhaps the ice absorbed us

[Motion's middle]

[Waving a lantern]

We can't go back

[After damp echoes]

[The balcony buried]

I thought I left it right here

[A violet note]

[To ask all the village clocks]

[It began with laughing]

A lagoon woman says:

If you are around when you go away

[Turn-fires twice lost]

That I saw

The selling of the sun

    [To die of a pattern]

        Just down the street

        Sonatine escapements

        Or the circle is not round

Found light in relation to   Or a finger touching itself

                    ⎡ Permanent spindles   ⎤

I might have suspected   It hardly ever rains

Underneath the skin   Because it's a wave

                    ⎣ The balustrade burning   ⎦

Used to see wind   Condensation of a mime

Always a thief's confession:

                :Hands holding the void
                :The of-waiting-to-be

Never said by the same voice:

                :Like dust's memory

There is no water reproduced:

                :Alone sounds
                :Which would be a room

We dressed as planets and twirled:

                :Eve of the longest day

Wheelman & the Painted Lady
Cradle themselves
In treetops above their graves

Cirrhosis of the giver

You can chew silence
Peeled like snow

Still hope
If a box has no sides

Considerate stones

An audible night you butterfly

Why twilight and dawn

Hangs in the far wall

Wind is born

Who can gainsay

The age of breath

Folded into fog

Freezing

Antic pillars

Words without limbs

Underswept

Partita

after Lutosławski

I am a lawyer because I have a fluent tongue, and am interested in legal subtleties; I am a stockbroker because my judgment of the markets is quick and sound; I am a professional batsman because I can hit unsually well. I agree that it might be better to be a poet or mathematician, but unfortunately I have no talent for such pursuits.

◊◊◊

Without mistakes life would be music.

Ad libitum 1

Yes, I envy those people who never existed.

◊◊◊

Menacing and peaceful forms. Probably this is the smoke of brush fires in the hollow. It might be the smoke of a burning house. Probably not a burning house. A bed in Majorca.

◊◊◊

Among European artistic circles and aristocracy in the 1800s, dying of consumption was widespread enough so as to be chic. Maternally-minded women flocked to the pale and delicate men, no more drawn in by their social standing or accomplishments than by the charisma of their cough.

Chopin's cough had particular sex appeal, or as Marie d'Agoult noted, he "coughed with unspeakable charm."

◊◊◊

Rain and the rhinoceros, obligatory parasites: all partings are equally sad, then water.

◊◊◊

To say nothing of the Greeks, or Joyce for that matter.

◊◊◊

It's too late to run away now. Like an arm through a window, the events of this week will bear me out.

◊◊◊

Blameless, perfect, etc., but I'd rather be wrong.

◊◊◊

A free-swinging pendulum gradually rotates.

◊◊◊

limited aleatorism or aleatorism of texture: the performers are given the freedom of establishing the order in which the formal elements, as composed by the author, are finally presented to the listeners. See also: *Conversation; Prayer; Marketing.*

◊◊◊

Mozart on Protestantism: "It's all in the head."

◊◊◊

An impression disguised as centuries.

◊◊◊

The only solution is to get smaller. If I keep getting smaller, I'll lose all size. When I lose my size, I'll become a zero; when I become a zero, I'll become everything.

◊◊◊

Anacleta, are you possessive?

Tone

for Agata Pietrasik

Impossible, this swept curve, sleep torn.

       Almost unguessable fractions, one
more rehearsal, impossible, purely so, curved in fog. Though not in any
strict sense, a door opens and goes on opening, impossible, to negotiate
the difference between a handshake and a poem. We all know dying in
Cleveland is

     redundant, yes, or maybe it's the weather. To just walk into
a photograph, impossible, sure, but plausible enough. And I'm grateful.
Impossible to marry my mailbox, impossible the curses this early. An
impossible affection for the same.

Ad libitum 2

There is no permanent place in the world
for ugly mathematics.

◊◊◊

As you know, I arrived in Buenos Aires on the liner *Chrobry* a week before
the war broke out.

◊◊◊

As you know, we've taken steps to institute an auction.

◊◊◊

After his death in Paris on October 17, 1849, and in keeping with the
composer's request, Chopin's heart was cut out and placed in a jar headed
for his homeland, Poland. Fearing it would be confiscated at the border by
the Russian government, Chopin's sister Ludwika hid his heart under her
dress — between her legs.

◊◊◊

A kiss, a continued fraction.

◊◊◊

They tend to let in some fresh air in one way, and in others they increase
the danger of suffocation by locking all the windows that look outward to
the world, or toward the sky.

◊◊◊

What the unity of intuition must.

◊◊◊

So many deformities crouching in all this, bathed regularly from the slate.

◊◊◊

Or else, think of the brain as a kind of spiritual lung.

◊◊◊

Gombrowicz, Witold (1904 – 1969). *A Guide to Philosophy in 6 Hours and 15 Minutes.* See also: *Diary; Ferdydurke; Cosmos; Pornographia; Trans-Atlantyk.*

◊◊◊

Individual events. Events beyond law. Events so numerous and uncoordinated that, flaunting their freedom from formula, they yet fabricate firm form.

◊◊◊

Can you answer a few questions about the precatory pea?

◊◊◊

True or False: Your lover thinks your pubic hair well-groomed.

◊◊◊

One could say, of course, this sort of thing puts us right next door to madness.

◊◊◊

Interior

after Lee Bontecou

So why this body again,   less inglorious,

                                        absorbed

in interminable games of patience. Why

            the doorbell once more, the
            anticipatory suspicion, why confess, why
            the hammer or lorry or spaceship?

    Why not mine or someone else's yellow expanding?

            Now you lag, tug, looking back, inescapable perhaps,
            no longer a mailbox to speak of.

    For the day, or a certain part of it, the rain slides.

    Prior architecture, the perfect colander:

Why not a candle, carpenter's bench, little hats and all manner of birds?

Part First——Chopin's Feet

I much prefer the Chopin that reaches me in the
street from an open window to the Chopin served
in great style from the concert stage.

Witold Gombrowicz, *Diary*

If it were not for and
don't stop to ask

I send you yesterday's ticket

12 études in 2 numbers

in vain
in the wall

Or what he called attempts

hung against light

not for such things
a slight case

not according to our meridian

out again, long

thinner still to transfer —

Now the face's furniture. That volute fall. Enveloped with either anatomy. Gasped silence. Instructions more equatorial.

The past of it. Too small. Possibly a whole house. A negative development of stars. These frozen weeks. Trapeze-shaped. Somewhat pale but present.

───────────────────────────────

Surround tables.
Severaled.
That still.
Slight graces shown without.

On your other neck.   On every other stairway negative sets.
A more complex permission.
                                                 A long ago if.
Midnight or next.   If you choose.
                                                 If slowly.

                                                 All the more so as showers.

Dotted today at tea

a slowly, grey octaves
so far as post

That is to say

three stairs expressed as an entire
afternoon

that indigo is not ether

not a sound
the wan smile of an errant comet

on the couch, bed

on reputation
with few appearances

First the partitions

wiping it off

The ones you entrusted
                few moments

against a list of streets

at the lightest
in contrary

Centuries as a private bath

an accidental precaution

I've composed nothing

That a waltz a whistle

into a second
both houses

As though this cough will

While you're resolving to find
faced with

in this unsweetly

I implore you

        second winter

a place to fold
scattered between them

Only begun unburned

A composition of pillars
A fallcoat
A longing for other cities

We met less and less often

As finger or floorboard

spitting basins full
quivering
or else with effort

One night to fold out

An arch-delicate
A perhaps table

Red clefts

Those palpable facts which

Never made of so many

Both arrived today
while staying at

no. 7 in C-sharp minor

Our   scented water
disconsolate

falling on the curtains

What might be carried in a jar

lain on top of light

  a brilliant
as to inscribe regret

I bowed, turned

Yet ourselves at each moment

  his catalogue
a forensic eloquence

It's very close now
unhurried

These tasks
         only cut shadows

Several keys so that

Although I have only.

Please send for.
Please copy my.

Don't present them until.

A thousand compliments.
A sharp breath.

All open but aspect

beyond rest or another thousand   The lower register
                                                              (unreflected)

these letters
a dish of coffee   a second sigh
                               gloves over any color

nervously guarded

in the direction of
in such a mood

late, if so

How he took the repeat

the palaced while

as if a chair
buried by lips

irresolutions

to variances

table into scales

that place of ragged correspondence

down worked

Or take something for your

just as night exhausts itself

at shoulder knots

at all elaborate

It was the silence that kept.
The vanish of the simplest givens.

Well-tailored.
Left between.
Bright fingers dangling.
The only informal you.

At my most unafraid,
diminished

the elbow asked for

if unspeakable charm
gravelblind

on vacancy

a limitation that makes
a principled avoidance

as with my habit of

the manifold yes
surface variations

your balcony a midnight

a necessary adjunct

split
recomposing caution

held, then only

After my treatment yesterday.
After oysters, at first course.

Symmetria (November)

Profitable silence is the measure of all things.
—Jacques Roubaud

How counting expressed it.

salt and cyan
lightbarrow
scarcely attenuated

might I simply pretend
for in the course, had come to

to bring scarves and apologies
speculative reason

no longer walking down

strange, another

and having to go back into it

fingers began to unpin

soon, an already waning
later, three chairs more ideally in rain

told into permanency

accorded a wall

If there's any improvement in your affairs
If your gesture's wrong

Author's Note

A number of works were crucial to the writing of this manuscript, either directly or indirectly, and I am no doubt greatly indebted to them. I wish to particulary acknowledge the following:

Diary and *Ferdydurke* by Witold Gombrowicz, *Conjectures of a Guilty Bystander* by Thomas Merton, *Night* by Verdana Rudan, *Lightduress* by Paul Celan, *A Mathematician's Apology* by G. H. Hardy, *The Man Who Knew Infinity* by Robert Kanigel, Gerhard Richter's paintings of rolls of toilet paper, Mark Rothko's *Seagram's Murals*, the work of Sean Scully and Lee Bontecou, *Polish Immigrants and Industrial Chicago* by Dominick Pacyga, the portraits of Stanisław Ignacy Witkiewicz, *Incompleteness* by Rebecca Goldstein, the nocturnes of Fryderyk Chopin, Witold Lutosławski, Roman Opałka, *Some Thing Black* by Jacques Roubaud, *Etat* by Anne-Marie Albiach, *The Revolution of Things* by Miron Białoszewski, *Deepstep Come Shining* by C. D. Wright, *Semiramis if I Remember* by Keith Waldrop, *Infinite in All Directions* by Freeman Dyson.

Biographical Note

Mark Tardi grew up in Chicago. Other publications include the chapbooks *Part First—Chopin's Feet* and *Airport music,* as well as the full length collection *Euclid Shudders.* He was a Fulbright Senior Lecturer in American Literature and Culture at the University of Łódź, Poland, and has translated, from the Polish, poetry by Kacper Bartczak, Miron Białoszewski, Monika Mosiewicz, and Przemysław Owczarek. He guest-edited a special issue of the literary journal *Aufgabe* devoted to Miron Białoszewski and contemporary Polish poetry and poetics.

This book was computer typeset in 10 pt. Palatino, with Lucida Casual titles and half-titles, by Rosmarie Waldrop. Printed on 60 lb. Nature's Recycled (an acid-free paper), smyth-sewn and glued into paper covers by McNaughton & Gunn in Saline, Michigan. There are 600 copies.